Lily Pads

ASHA BIANCA

WESTBOW
PRESS®
A DIVISION OF THOMAS NELSON
& ZONDERVAN

WestBow Press books may be ordered through booksellers or by contacting:

WestBow Press
A Division of Thomas Nelson & Zondervan
1663 Liberty Drive
Bloomington, IN 47403
www.westbowpress.com
1 (866) 928-1240

ISBN: 978-1-9736-3667-0 (sc)
ISBN: 978-1-9736-3666-3 (e)

Print information available on the last page.

WestBow Press rev. date: 8/20/2018

People are placed in our lives by God like lily pads on the pond of life. The journey across becomes more beautiful and possible because of each of these steps pathed along the way. Some gentle, some rough, each one can be turned into a divine appointment with the eternal perspective.

Jump on in to my fifth book and let's talk about the people who make up a tribe and how to see God's light in every situation.

To Chelsea, E, T & My Tribe -
Thank you for loving me so
deeply, fairly and rightly. I
am a better mom, human and
woman because of each of you.

Contents

Introduction
Lily pads

People, the ones who hold, harm and help us along the way. Each person in our life is placed by God, like a lily pad across the pond of our life. Even if God wouldn't choose the person who we choose, He can help us navigate our choices in any situation. Whether a person is placed for us to learn from them or love them deeply, each and every relationship has something to teach us.

Each and every relationship has something to teach us.

God loves us each in a way that is so hard to even fathom. He knows that while we are on this earth, we can encourage and edify one another in powerful ways. He also knows that we can tear one another down with one word or action. This gift and responsibility of relationship is one that is tough to master.

This gift and responsibility of relationship is one that is tough to master.

This relationship balance is one of the reasons I am in awe of Jesus and how he lived his life on earth. He was 100% God and 100% Human, which means he must have had moments of being fairly annoyed with people. He had the same feelings as we do and managed to control them, speak truth and love well in spite of those feelings. Circumstances did not rock his ability to trust in God or love people well.

Once while co-facilitating a grief share course, I realized that even though Jesus knew all that was and all that would be, he felt deeply and even mourned. This became more clear to me when we talked about Lazarus's death. Jesus knew that He would be raising him back to life, however Jesus still wept. This hit me right in the gut, if the God of the universe grieved with knowing every "why" and every "what" that could possible be, the power of relationships is a really important lesson to lean into.

The power of relationships is a really important lesson to lean into.

Lily pads is my last of a five book series. This series of therapeutic discovery books started with random thoughts, rounding into esteem and identity struggles, circled with a second mighty random, then most recently navigating the gray between the black and white of issues and rests here at Lily pads. Lily pads is a book that is truly an end point of journeying through this writing discovery and following God's lead.

Well, let's start with the basics, I love writing. Truly, it is one of those activities that fuels me. I'm tucked right now in my tiny home writing this sentence and filled to the brim with joy. There is something about the written word that reminds me it is ok to pause, reflect, guess, not know the answer, hope. All of these responses are a-ok. There is something free'ing in knowing that I can edit, alter, reread and express myself through words. Speaking is something I do for my work, however writing is something I do for myself.

> *Speaking is something I do for my work, however writing is something I do for myself.*

Writing is also an indulgence to me, to take an hour today and work on this intro feels like I'm eating a whole bar of chocolate! The gift of self-love time that these five books have given me is priceless. The books are not perfect and I would write them each differently at different points in time than I did. I disagree with some statements that I have made and could have definitely included more, reduced certain parts. However, they are all mine, as a gift to you and an offering to my creator, mistakes and all!

So let's dig in and walk through how God has placed people into my life as Lily pads. I hope you see how He has and is doing similarly throughout your journey as well!

Chapter 1
Roots

Roots are the wings to our lives. Roots help us know where we came from and in the most functional families offer support as we branch out on our own. Without solid roots, the growth will be shallow and the tree will be at risk of being uprooted. Several times in my life I have felt uprooted and then remember the might oak of God who strengthens every single root, ensuring it is secure for the moment when it is most needed. Some families do the uprooting, some families, root and never allow for growth and some families are masters of developing roots and wings. Whichever you come from, it's not too late to develop both. We'll walk through a bit of my roots in this chapter.

There are different thoughts about families and how we end up in one. Some who believe in reincarnation, say children pick their parents. This is an interesting theory however not one I adopted. There was a child who my parents conceived before me who didn't make it because they weren't ready. I always wondered about what life would have been like with this sibling. However, that wasn't to be. I think one day in heaven, I might meet her or him and it will be a great reunion, however until then it is what it is.

So to start from the beginning, I arrived on a fall day in Paradise, California to two people committed to me and to each other in a fairly unconventional way. They never ended up marrying, which was most likely for the best. My mom already had two boys, one 10 and one 13 and I was the first child for my dad. My parents named me Asha Bianca meaning white light. Turns out Asha would have been my name whether I was male or female. Asha is a game of chance from eastern India that they played on occasion. I've learned Asha also means hope, I've grown to love my name. I am very glad that I am a girl though, Asha was rough enough growing up without being a boy with this name.

Childhood is an interesting experience, so unique, no two are alike.

Childhood is an interesting experience, so unique, no two are alike.

My parents gave it their best to live communally for a couple years, living together without driving each other completely crazy. Then my mom moved into the garage workshop area and my dad and I stayed up in the main house until that no longer worked. I remember reading this children's book in that little nook that she had been in about a woman who was a mother. The visual stuck with me, the woman was strong, she was carrying two bags of groceries with a baby next to her and one in a holder on her. I imprinted on this book. There was one other book I read often in the place where my mom used to sleep, it was about Queen Anne's Lace. I still love this weed, to me it is the most beautiful weed there is. I read those two books hundreds of times.

I'm not sure how else to describe my childhood except, different. There were two other small studios on my dad's land and one of them became mine, the other his. He loved me well, through listening and kindness. Material items were not a part of our world, we lived simply. It was rare to have a Christmas tree, instead of the lights on the ficus tree. Most years the gifts under the tree were essentials, face cream, socks, shoes, his hugs and presence were the best present. He tried hard to always get at least one big gift, such as a new pair of sneakers. The carpet was made up of carpet sample squares so every one was different in texture and design.

My mom's love was more of a rush that flew in with different gifts and energy in spades. She would bring people into the space she was in until that didn't work well for her or them. She would send gifts, leaves and post cards of her adventures. I kept those post cards for a long time. She was building sand sculptures all over the world and staying in one zip code wasn't really the life of a gypsy, which she truly is. Her homes were temporary, however she made great beds. The covers were laid just so and pillows for days. She also hung pots and pans on the walls, I loved the accessibility of them and way they looked. During one particular earthquake, the sound and shaking is etched in my memory. I don't remember any time my parents were together, however I also don't remember anytime they spoke poorly of one another. They were determined to their own lives and I would be a part of each of them. My mom can also make dinner literally out of anything in the cupboards. We once went on a month long rice and beans adventure and the day there was feta for a topping was a good day. There were a couple traditions upheld, mom generally moved once a year. It became clear after kindergarten that it was going to make more sense to live at my dad's. My mom lived in the area until I was in jr. high then I don't remember seeing her as much. I lived briefly with her my freshman year of high school, however she was chasing a man who didn't seem good for any one.

One tradition of my mom's had been to sneak to my dad's house in the middle of the night and pick me up to go pick up my friends for ice cream and Denny's. Sometimes dad was home, other times he wasn't. It was an adventurous feeling to be at a playground on the swings in the middle of the night. Generally my friends were boys so we picked up one friend and his cousin who were both large samoans and whose parents didn't seem to mind, which I never thought of until now.

One tradition of my dad's had been to fly to Chicago every year and visit his family there. The house they lived in had three floors, still only twin beds for us to sleep in and the smell of white bread with thick butter from my grandpa in the morning, mounds of it. My great grandparents lived above them, and a great aunt above them. There were grape vines terraced about in a small background of concrete. The places I remember the most activity however, was my grandpa in the garage, my grandma in the kitchen and this little sitting room where everything was covered with plastic with orange candies. We weren't allowed to eat them, although I'm certain I did. I was a bit of a rebel that way. My California upbringing rubbed my grandma and aunts wrong on more than one occasion. I remember being at an ice cream stand and asking for a different flavor. There was a long conversation about children being meant to be seen not heard. I understood why my dad didn't live there anymore. He loved them, however he had grown bigger than the twin bed and just didn't fit quite right anymore. My dad would take me to some friend's houses, Crystal with a y and i both, one was filled with Mexican cooking yum, the other with the smiths playing in the air. My dad bought these heart stickers that he would share with my class on occasion and bring ice cream, it was quite the treat.

My mom generally lived communally. My mom was also sort of like a magnet, strong talented and creating strong attraction or resistance with all she met. This meant that I was always meeting diverse interesting people. I loved dipping buttered toast into hot chocolate with my mom. She also told stories with this exuberance that was one of a kind. She is still the most talented person who I have ever met. She didn't get on well with some people and others was inseparable for chapters of time. I didn't listen very well and challenged her often. It was a bit too much I think. I read a quote by Maya Angelou, included below that sums my mother up well.

that many envy. He too, had his own battles, he is wiser than most. I'm thankful to say that I am writing this section, flying to Hawaii to celebrate his 50th birthday, what a gift he is. I ask him tough questions now, when I'm not sure what to do. He says things straight and true like an arrow, sometimes it feels like he is shooting them at you. He doesn't mean to, he has no time or space for nonsense, after dealing with too much of it. Sometimes I forget that he is who he is with a raw wit, and then I remember. He loves big but exclusively, it is a gift to be one of the few in his circle. Glad to be in that circle, I love him so.

He has no time or space for nonsense, after dealing with too much of it.

Chapter 2
WOW

Adolescence was tricky for me. If you've read my book Sex Esteem, you'll know that I began finding my identity in boys then men, way too early. Right around twelve, to be exact. It became a cycle that created trouble beyond my years or maturity level. Basically, I ran amuck.

I remember the first time innocence leaked out, I was at one of the places my mom and I were staying, in a little cottage far from anywhere. She wasn't with me at the time, she was probably working and there were videos in a bookcase. Two bookshelves full of videos, all with story tale names like Snow White, Cinderella, etc. I played one expecting to watch a sweet show and found it was not the kind of movie that I was expecting. Instead of the PG movies I was expecting, the shelves were filled to the brim with porn. I couldn't have been much older than 10 and remember the fascination of stumbling into something new and beyond me. The foothold was open and visuals had taken seed, it was a pivotal moment in my body image life. The sketchy side took control and at one point I was almost trafficked due to my exposure and willingness to seek love in the worst kind of hiding places.

Many years later, these experiences are some of the reasons why I now serve as a volunteer leader fighting against human trafficking. God knew that I needed this volunteer cause effort to help restore the little girl in me who was exposed to darkness too soon.

> *God knew that I needed the volunteer cause effort to help restore the little girl in me who was exposed to darkness too soon.*

Many people want to know more about the anti-human trafficking efforts. There are hundreds of amazing organizations across the world, working as safe houses to shelter and restore. At my church, we have a set me free shop that displays products from around the world that are made by survivors of trafficking. One of my favorite products that we have in the set me free shop is a shirt that shows the first time a rescued woman learns how to write her name. It has her name written over and over again. It is a beautiful reminder of our identity and worth!

Some interested people ask what are practical actions to fight against this $150 billion monster business of human trafficking, there are many, here's my top 5 suggestions of where to start:

1) Stop porn.
2) Pause to value human life and worth in every circumstance.
3) Educate yourself on the topic, Feb 22nd is end slavery day for instance. There are many days similar to this one, start researching.
4) Do something, no matter how small. Read an article, pickup a letter template to send to the government.
5) Hope & Pray for a new day when the atrocities that occur in the dark are no longer allowed in our world. One freedom story at a time. I became lost in the world of myself. Now I help to point others to being free, God is good.

Right around my later teens, I got pregnant with the first of two incredible gifts that God has given me. I had dodged being pregnant many times before, I remember a middle school counselor talking with me after a scare.

There was something that shifted in me the first time I held my first child, I was forever changed. She was the most perfect thing I had ever seen and I loved her instantly! To describe the honor of being a mom is something that I'll have to do better when I get to heaven, for now this is the closest that I can come to the honor.

Before I was a mom:
I thought of myself first.
Average sleep % was way up.
Cheering for others was an underdeveloped talent.
My heart had not broken for someone else.
Going to work was optional.
How much God loves me was theoretical.
Of all the titles that I have, this one is my favorite.

To great women out there raising beautiful people; you have a most important joy, celebrate the gift of teaching them that they are so loved, embrace the exhaustion as the brief season of time that it is, and know that you can support them 100% financially and emotionally if you are single. If God happens to give you the blessing of a wonderful providing husband who is a father to them, love him so well, appreciate him. Do not belittle him or criticize him. Know that God has wired him as a dad and that looks differently than a mom but is critically important. Esteem him in front of your children, always. Do not let your children disrespect him in any way. Confront disagreements in the private moments with just you and him, however stand united with him in front of your kids.

One caution, if things aren't right at home and you think that you are keeping it all together and compensating for abusive behavior, stop right now. Seek therapy, pray fiercely, call a spade a spade, be honest with your children about what is and is not acceptable and seek help for your family without sweeping unhealthy detrimental and abusive behaviors under the rug.

embrace the exhaustion as the season of time that it is

To the great women who haven't yet realized the incredible responsibility and honor of having a child, who take them for granted and speak harshly to them, please stop. One of my hardest memories to forgive is a very harsh look I would receive when someone who was supposed to love me would give me when they were hurting, that look was etched in my identify for a long time. The responsibility of being a parent is not one to take lightly. Done well, it is the best gift ever. However, handled with neglect or mistrust and the scars are deep. Treat it seriously, those little ears and eyes are watching. What you say about them, they feel deep inside them. It doesn't mean you have to sugar coat correction, however it does mean believing and encouraging the best in them while providing a safe nurturing space for them where they know you have their back is key.

Please stop.

If you haven't been the best parent, which at times is all of us. If you haven't sought forgiveness and come clean with areas that you think you could have done better.

Right this moment, stop in your tracks and no matter how old your children are, tell them you are sorry with tears in your eyes and pray for God to help you be a more loving, nurturing and supportive mother. It is one of those jobs that is not seen by most and falls into the category of doing the right thing even when no one is watching, they are watching and feeling and learning who they are and what is acceptable from you.

My daughter is one of the most forgiving people who I have ever met. When I came to her and said that I really should have done better, she met this hard conversation with such grace and love, it was a complete gift. Even if your child doesn't forgive as easily, make yourself vulnerable, be genuine and sincere. Then you will be able to hold your head high and move on knowing that you don't have to be captive by the past. Take every opportunity to make the future a great one. Be extra kind, be extra loving, pray for that child and pray for your relationship to strengthen. God is the best restorer and no relationship is beyond his miraculous power.

It just has to be said. If you don't want to put this kind of energy into this critical role, simple, then don't create a child. If you have a child, then be the best mom or dad that you can be, period.

> *If you don't want to put this kind of energy into this critical role, simple, then don't create a child.*

Chapter 3
Survival

Trust is tough for me, granted I didn't necessarily learn to trust very well. There were ups and downs as I grew up and sometimes it felt like I was more on my own than I should have been. This led to fumbling through relationships in an odd way, without knowing healthy and unhealthy as acutely as would have been helpful. I'm not sure I knew what to expect from my marriage, not really seeing any healthy women and men relationships other than on tv. Needless to say I read a quote recently that summed up my existence for the majority of my marriage, "When one is surviving they can't dream." There were moments when the words seemed real and when the actions seemed like they would come however another quote that I love, "The best apologize is changed behavior," never came to fruition.

I learned a great deal from my marriage and from being single again. The lesson I learned from my marriage is to run to God in absolutely everything. The discipline of feeling completely trapped, hopeless, and afraid created a response that I was either going to run to drugs, alcohol, other men - none of which

I could live with for my children's sake, so I ran into faith, and leaned into the hardest moments with resolve to believe the best. When I felt certain that it wasn't going to end well, I went to a Christian therapist and learned about boundaries, strategies, how valuable I was a part from just a pay check. I learned how to be a woman, this was and continues to be new territory.

Some of the lessons that I learned about marriage is that someone can value you more for money than your heart. This has been a constant focus of mine is to not get caught-up in the money of this world. After all, all money is God's anyway. One of my early pastors, taught me about tithing and I have never looked back. Put simply, you just can't out give God. God will honor me for turning to his lead for wisdom and honoring him with every good gift from above. This is where faith and kingdom perspective come in. Some of my closest friends and confidents tithe consistently no matter the circumstances, they know that it is all God's anyway. They model what it means to pay off a house early, support their children well through college, budget responsibly and always give God what is his first.

After all, all money is God's anyway.

I learned about the reality of God one long drive with my God dad, he fought relentlessly for my soul the way only an appointment with the holy spirit can. We spent hours sparring through so many different sides of faith. He was patient, honest and in the end the power of faith won. The calm, presence that had been with me always, called white light, now known as God changed my life forever. I remember one particularly amazing time when I felt the holy spirit lead me, I was on a muni in San Francisco. I was a freshman attending my first couple weeks of high school at an art academy. I had stayed too late at school and boarded late at night, already a bad idea. There were two individuals heavily intoxicated and they began to heckle me. I was all of 14 and knew I was in a bad situation. I was turned to them and they were about to touch my shoulder when I heard the still small voice say, "pretend to be hearing impaired." I instantly began to sign the alphabet in sign language. I had learned it in school. Their whole demeanor changed, they began talking kindly to me and helped me figure out when my stop would be. The power and protection of that still small voice kept me safe that night and many others.

We spent hours sparring through many different sides of faith.

It was beautiful and I never turned back. Once I found that comfort of the only true comforter, there was never another way for me. God has truly comforted me through every step of my life so far, whether divorce or being laid off or medical concerns with my loved ones. Divorce has been hard, mostly because of sharing time with our children, it is the reason I waited so long and tried so hard not to divorce. However, the authenticity by being real, safe and not trying to take on the world without truth and love has been the right decision, over and over again. I have earnestly tried to not air the hard world of my past and because of this attempt, I remember my wise friend telling me, "If you chose not to share about the whys, people are not going to understand and you're going to have to be ok with that."

The in's and outs of a volatile relationship are so private that trust me you never know what is going on behind closed doors, no matter what it looks like from the outside. My normal was not a normal by any means. It took a long time until I recognized my value, worth and what was no longer negotiable.

One of my most loyal hiking and praying friends explained that she always knew something was off and had to let me figure it out for myself. This was wisdom as well, my denial was deep and long. I was afraid for a long time.

The in's and outs of a volatile relationship are so private that trust me you never know what is going on behind closed doors, no matter what it looks like from the outside.

For those of you contemplating divorce, please do try everything in your power to stay in your marriage. The pain and hardships that come from divorce are just a different hard and there is always hope when both you and your spouse are willing to give it your all. Start by getting over yourself and the idea that you can do it all by yourself. God is the only way to save your marriage, lean into him with your spouse. Make love everyday even if you don't feel like it. Speak kindly and be their best friends, as well as biggest advocate. Know that you left every single try on the mat before you give up. I promise you life won't be a bed of roses after you are divorce, just different thorns. Choose wisely and do not ever dishonor your children or spouse by giving up without a true fight.

Know that you left every single try on the mat before you give up.

For those on the other side of divorce, grace is real. Divorce is hard, the best description I've heard of it is from Mr. Fred Rogers. He wrote, "Divorce is like a piece of clothing being torn. It's never the same no matter how we try to mend it back together."

Grace is real.

I've had almost 5 years experience with this torn garment once this book is published, not a place I'd ever thought I'd be but none-the-less, here I am.

Below are some of the things I've learned and tips for others navigating these stormy waters:

1) Don't take sides, things like only liking one person's posts ever, cheering only one on in life, talking badly about the other. The truth is you'll never know truly what happened behind closed doors and guaranteed you don't have the whole story. If either person has any integrity you'll know very little of the story, ever.

2) Kids come first, no matter what. Being kind to both parents shows this to be true. Believe me kids notice everything.

3) If you had a strong relationship pre divorce with in-laws chances are you still will. If not, they gone, faster than you can believe it. Let them go, no matter how much you've done for them, how long you were in their lives, and what they turned a blind eye to. Let them go.

4) Divorce is not the unforgivable sin. Stop pretending you're a judge in someone else's life. The consequences and suffering of divorce are self-contained. There is restoration and healing possible always through God but not easily.

5) Life's not fair and generally neither are terms of divorce, be extra kind.

6) If you have a question, ask the source. Don't talk about other's stories.

7) I am a whole woman without a man; if it takes me awhile to trust and commit be ok with that. God is enough.

8) Life will feel uncertain, fear not, grow your faith and know nothing can separate you from the will of God.

9) Again if you can stay, do. Marriage is a union that should be protected fiercely. If you can reunite, do. With two people fighting for their marriage who surrender to God anything is possible.

10) Realize you're not alone, there are others who have walked through this land, survived and are thriving. There are others who have hope and joy in their lives abundantly. God is with you, ask for his help and be encouraged.

Realize you're not alone, there are others who have walked through this land, survived and are thriving.

The other area of my life that had its fair share of survival was my work. It's ironic as I complete the final edit of this book I was just laid off last week, after going on 22 years with the same employer. I love what my dear friend said to me, "Asha, your track record is 100% when overcoming adversity and this will be no different." Pure gold right there, a friend like that.

I started early with work, and haven't stopped yet. I began buying my own things right around the age of 13. I got emancipated at 15 and started the last job I had a first day at when I was 19, with a 9 month old. I had survived up until last week in this career, although it had not been a cake walk.

When one of my wise friends was praying for me last week, she thanked God that I survived in this career in corporate America for that long due to his provision, my integrity and honest hard work. It is incredible the way God has blessed my career and the fierce coworkers that I am thankful to call friends. They have known me in a way few have, they have challenged me in great ways and we have survived together in many ways. You see at work, I had no real fear compared to home, it was my escape in many ways and I loved it. As much as I would have preferred to be a stay at home mom for my kids, I am grateful for the story God is telling with my outside work as well.

They have known me in a way few have...

Unfortunately, many teams have been reorganized in this new day and age of needing higher margin. It has been tough to watch people who you walked through halls with, met about ideas on and generally worked towards a common good, walk out. There are way too many to list, but they know who they are. They're my people and always will be. It has been a total grieving being on the other side of that packet as well. The investment, trust, time and heart that took years to build and moments to be over. It really is like nothing I have ever experienced. The most powerful part is that God was with me the entire day, I just knew something was off and when I was told that my position was eliminated, I didn't see red, instead I thanked the team members for what had been an incredible career. I had the most important information ready for them to ensure the business, more specifically my team and clients were as well off as it could be under these circumstances. God was with me every moment. He was there when I texted my two best friends and they showed up in my driveway at the same moment. He was there when my son had incredible support as well, and we prayed together on my bed. I will never forget those moments.

Interns sometimes have asked for advice, here's my top shelf with brevity:

Never talk negatively about others, say it to them and only them.

If you must escalate make sure you have met 4 many 1 on 1's.

Do the hard thing first, fast and right.

Never let it be about the pay check.

Do what you ask your team to do.

Give more than you think you can or should, credit will sort itself out.

Show up, be brave and keep your word.

Show up, be brave and keep your word.

As I think back on the loads of talented courageous people who I have met throughout my career, I see God's hand on each one placed in my path and I am thankful. So as I look for my next career chapter, I am eager to study, learn, challenge and negotiate in new ways through dreaming instead of merely surviving.

It seems logical the tv show that I have watched most in my life, is Survivor. I almost went on it once, I made it to the final round and learned that I was pregnant with my second child. I call him my million dollar baby. He was a complete miracle and truly a second gift from God. I don't have many regrets in life, I chose the right thing with God's help more than I didn't. However, if I could have named my second born after my eldest brother, I would do it over and over again. I gave in when I shouldn't have. I've learned that my voice is worth just as much as anyone's, no matter how much louder theirs is.

I've learned that my voice is worth just as much as anyone's, no matter how much louder theirs is.

Beautiful moment happened about a month ago when my daughter and her husband chose to name their first born with her uncle's name to honor him. No words, just a lot of tears when they made this decision. Life goes on and sometimes the gift is even sweeter the second time choices are made.

Remember to have some fun when you are outwitting, outplaying and outlasting on whichever survival expedition that you are currently on!

Chapter 4
Serve

I have a high energy level. I can go and go and go, until I get so tired. Generally the first sign that I am tired, is I drop things. This high energy level has been helpful for redirecting some of the frustrations in my life towards a greater good. When my children were young, I couldn't bear to work all day and then pass them off to a youth worker, so I stayed. I stayed every Wednesday and am still staying on Wednesdays to serve with youth. I fight that awkward feeling of being too old, not cool enough, all that bologna every single time.

I fight that awkward feeling of being too old, not cool enough, all that bologna every single time.

However, I stay, I show-up and I listen every moment that I can. I have had children tell me such hard things and it has been an honor to show them God's love, acceptance and be there without judgement on them. We can learn so much from children and youth if we approach these nights with humility. It wasn't long before the kids knew that I had to study the verses also, because I hadn't grown up in church the way many of them had.

I had the kids pray for each other often, something about them learning how to pray out loud or in their hearts helped them to know they have a voice and God is listening. God is there for all of them no matter their size, for the little child who wanted to come home with me when I volunteered at an orphanage in Mexico to the babies who I have held in Haiti.

The process of letting free burdens and praying fiercely is very active as a youth leader, relying on God to intervene where you can't make the impact you'd like and trusting that every walking being is loved by Him. This truth helps you see them through His eyes and feel their need through His provision. It also helps with the impact that you can make to ensure you know that your small word, action or prayers helped pull someone closer to God.

Your small word, action, or prayers helped pull someone closer to God.

I've had the opportunity to speak to women several times through out God's calling through service. It is a treasure to share my heart with women who are lost in a way that I can relate to. One of the tenderest women who I have met, shared with me that the key to a strong marriage is to serve beside your husband, I loved this visual of walking hand in hand to serve God. It is a prayer of mine.

Other countries have a big place in my heart as well. I have a God Son in Colombia who I love the same as if I birthed him. I'll never forget when he was graduating from high school, I told him that I could send $500 or come visit for one day. He told me he wanted me to come visit for one day and see him graduate. That boy's heart, he was placed in my life by God to show how much you can love someone who wasn't family until you met and then you just know, he's yours.

I've traveled to Haiti, and Southeast Asia with many more countries on my list. The heartache and hardship can seem more than any person can bear, however you watch how their resilience and faith is so strong. I find myself coming back from trips over and over again believing that we in America have too much comfort to rely on God the way those less wealthy do. When an individual is praying for a meal and it shows up day after day in a miraculous was, their faith grows in a supernatural way. When an individual watches their child die and suffer more than any parent can take and runs to God for healing it is a true miracle how they can be comforted in the midst of the unthinkable.

More than any parent can take and runs to God for healing it is a true miracle.

If you are ever able to go on a missions trip, I would highly recommend it. Know that you are making a difference by showing a group of whoever God places in your steps that you care. You care enough to show-up, pray, meet them and share yourself with them.

If you prefer to give donations, be so generous and try not to fret over this and that way an organization uses what, give it to God and trust that He will direct it where it needs to be. An old saying was, "Where will we get the money from" and the wise one said, "from wherever it is right now." I love this! God isn't short of cash and He will bless your givings like he did the young child's sack lunch to feed thousands!

Where will we get the money from?

From wherever it is right now.

Below is a summary of the trip this year with a local group that leads business with mission expeditions:

40hrs of flight time, 25hrs of driving, 15-7 year olds singing you raise me up, 12 passenger vans, 8 flights in 9 days, 8 visits, 7 mornings of 3am wake-ups, 5 Safe House visits, 4 paintings by elephants, 3 times eating dessert first, 2 dozen cups of coffee, a gang of tigers, 2 lions & 1 belly rub, 1 police stop, buckets of fish, 1 tub filled with hopeful honest work, a blind angel's serenade, 0 phone calls, Aussies & Canadians, 42 bomb deaths last year, not enough rose apples eaten, endless courageous colleagues, some laughs & some tears, rescued daughters & sons, new friends, thousands of prayers.

Best movie - Walter Mitty, Best food - Zion's cafe, Best book - The Bible.

Experience = priceless.

If you are able to physically serve, do it. There will never be another more gratifying experience. Pray about the best organization, place or area to serve and go for it. I think as a country we tend to be pretty self focused, service is the best antidote to this way of thinking. Getting yourself out of your own head and jumping into another's world through moments is a true gift.

I have the honor to serve as a chaplain through my church. It is an intense and gratifying service assignment. The confidentiality required and reliance on God is key. A critical point is to know when you are over your head in a situation, remembering it's not about you.

Knowing when you are over your head in a situation. Remember it's not about you.

Many times I have just read the word of God until I was ready to pray. I have prayed with many people, people who have just learned that they have terminal cancer, lost loved ones, deep pain, God is in every single circumstance and there to provide comfort when asked.

I recently had a very hard experience, with my first grandson having to be in the NICU right after birth. Every step of the process was traumatic and I have a new respect for parents and families with hurt or sick loved ones. The first three nights I read the bible out loud until I could make my way to the chapel then I prayed on my knees, then it got easier to pray out loud and in the shower and lean into my almighty God.

Here are a few excerpts that I wrote while going through this part of our journey both inside the hospital and surrounded by love outside as well:

Today…early this morning I kissed my grand boy and headed to the outdoor garden on floor 8 of the hospital River wing where Mt. Rainier climbed above the fog and peeked into my view. I knew I needed some air, to smell flowers, and a plan. I knew I wanted to get their house in order in case my daughter and her family could go home from the hospital this week.

I knew I needed to get clothes, medicine, a list of items that they couldn't have predicted needing a week + 1 day ago. I knew their mailbox was full and boxes from moving in just over a month ago were outside the door. I knew I needed a good night's sleep and a tub before driving back to the hospital tomorrow.

However, I didn't know the huge blessing that awaited me when dear friends KNOCKed it out of the park with and for me. Seriously though, below is the list that they blessed us with today.

Many hands make light work and woes lighter, indeed.

- homemade enchiladas
- cookies to knock your socks off
- built a dresser, yes I said built
- mowed the lawn
- put together a super swanky pack & play, 2x
- diaper genie set-up
- folded & hung literally dozens of clothes by size
- vacuumed
- put together bath tub with toys
- played soccer outside
- did laundry
- trimmed the bushes
- played hide and seek
- cleaned
- no nonsense
- built styrofoam forts

- laughed
- listened
- smiled
- shared
- hugged
- loved well

This morning I felt a twang sad that I was going to miss church, tonight in the tub I realize I felt church all day.

I felt church all day.

So the NICU, now that my grand boy's attending physician has said the words "possibility of home" in today's daily rounds, not words said lightly here, I wanted to share a little about this place as we may get to go to their house within the next week or two, granted all goes ok in the next 5 minutes and the 5 minutes after that.

So...

Time stands still in here, there is nothing more important than the next breath, test result, medicine dose, round update.

Time stands still in here

Time is also a constant thought that you hold and suppress in one swift action. The back of your mind starts with will we bring them home ever, then will it be years, then will it be months, then weeks...you get it however, you also realize none of it is in your control so you focus on pump times every three hours, am and pm medicine doses, the next activity and not a step ahead for fear it changes yet again and that feeling of ok deep breath two steps backward can be avoided.

Energy is a top commodity, sleep in itself and a plan for sleep with your team makes or breaks you when you receive any news.

People are going through so much and because of it there is this atmosphere of grace and patience that we breath with each other.

Atmosphere of grace and patience that we breath with each other.

On the sleeping floor where families come from all over the world for care, no one asks how you're doing, no one says much of anything, they smile softly or turn to cry in private, they hold the door for you and look at you in the eyes and you all just know. It's so beautiful and powerful.

Emotional intelligence is the number one skill the top nurses and doctors have. The way they provide candid purposeful communication when they are really on their game is a sight to be seen, let me tell you. Lack of emotional intelligence hits you in the gut and it takes a lot of self control not to scream at someone who says something so off, given the circumstances. But, you don't, you breath deep, cry in the shower and lock arms with your team.

But, you don't, you breath deep, cry in the shower and lock arms with your team.

Keeping each other focused on the positive and celebrating the small wins is what every day consists of to keep the stamina up. Constant communication about breathing, pooping, feeding, levels of this, behaviors of that.

Support is indescribable, a text, a prayer, a call, a photo, a question even if the answer is we don't know, an ask about a visit even if they're not ready for visitors yet, a team member saying I got X you focus on Y. Support is indescribable. When my sister brought us clothes, snacks and love. When my brother brought the bear book, no words for how important these moments are.

There is joy and grief in the same moment all the time. Our first 24 hours here a newborn lost its fight and one went home. Our hearts have powerful beats encompassing all emotions intertwined without lessening the volume of any of them.

Our hearts have powerful beats encompassing all emotions intertwined without lessening the volume of any of them.

Only if you're a breastfeeding mom is the food good, they have their own chef, so smart.

The vending machines break often. Usually when you are most hungry.

The chapel is the best place to "get away".

5 minutes outside feels like 2 days. 1 day inside feels like 5 days.

Every single person is trying their best.

Whether you're onsite or far away, there are never enough answers.

Whether you're onsite or far away, there are never enough answers.

You forget so many things, like to eat, where your water bottle is, what day it is.

What day it is

There is a new respect for those who have experienced what you are experiencing and all of a sudden you are part of a club that no one would choose to join.

You are part of a club that no one would choose to join.

How God places people in your life like Lily pads across the pond journey of your life ♥.

Chapter 5
Freedom

There is a photo of me at the beach, that embodies freedom. I must be about 8 and I'm looking straight in the camera with such joy in my eyes. When I look at this photo, I remember the little girl in me who believed she could do anything and be anyone. She is grit, hope, and raw Asha. It is a special photo. It reminds me that we only place limits on ourselves through our hurts and walls that we build to protect ourselves. Freedom is trusting in a God that is mightier than the deepest hurt. Protecting ourselves is important. Forgiving without allowing unhealthy patterns to continue is essential. Living scared is not.

God is mightier than the deepest hurt.

The woods also feel like freedom to me, the beautiful creator has a delightful surprise at every turn. This world is not heaven but it is a taste of His masterpiece as an artist.

Sounds of freedom

I love the way the following list of sounds are the truth that allow me to be free in my faith:

Waves crashing
Leaves against the wind
Baby giggles
Deep belly laughs
The gasp of trying something new, like jumping out of plane with your nephew
The applause at the end of when authenticity and justice prevail

Actions of Freedom

I love the way the following list of actions are the truth that allow me to be free in my faith:

A genuine hug
hands holding
piggy-back rides
watching my dad dance or roller skate
watching my mom paint or carve
watching my brothers and nephews surf
my daughter & son talking with their newborn
dancing anywhere
praying anywhere
my sister making coffee

Scents of Freedom

I love the way the following list of scents are the truth that allow me to be free in my faith:

fresh baked bread, cookies and cakes
cut grass by man who cherishes you
grilling salmon
bon fires
roses
lavender
coconut
baby oil
red velvet cake baked on my brother's birthday
salt water

The people who have given me the best freedom and purpose in life are my children, they are the world to my heart and my purpose. One day if God would have me marry the man who gives me piggy back rides across finish lines, that will be a new #2 commitment right under God but for right now, it's all about my kids.

My first born
She can make me laugh no matter what. She is the most forgiving human I have ever met. She can make any situation fun. She is the life of any party. To hear her laugh, is a truly unique experience. She is fiercely for me. When she first met the man I am dating, she put her finger right in his chest and

said, "if you ever hurt my mom, I'll kill you." This woman can handle really anyone and anything. She has a heart of gold, knows who she is and isn't afraid of what you think of her. She makes me courageous every time I'm with her and I love the person who she is. She calls me her best friend. There are no words for how much I love her and there is nothing I wouldn't do for her. The way she looks at her husband and baby makes me know she is a woman after God's own heart.

She is my world.

My second born

He was a miracle from the start, said to be not possible and then there he was. He has been the easiest child I have ever met, kind, sweet and just. As a teen he's full of sass & spunk but chooses his moments. He keeps this momma in check daily and hugs me like he's going to crush me. He loves hanging with his friends and this new taste of freedom as a sophomore. His music preferences are diverse enough to make him a super DJ on our car rides and if I by chance have the aux, he's the decider of which to skip (anything country) and which to replay (currently drake and so many others I've never heard). The questions he asks me, oh wow, especially when his buddies are over, just wow. He has an integrity, fairness and wisdom that makes me stop in my tracks and pay attention to this awesome gift of him. He has this cool about him without even trying and gets me like few do. He snuggles most with me during worship at church and loves God. He recently spoke in front of the entire congregation about his faith, it may have been my favorite moment so far as his mom. We speak Spanish when we are at restaurants, just the two of us, it's our thing. El mundo de mi vida, the world to my life, thankful.

My Son In Love

She smiled when she talked about him, that was the first good sign. He was eager to meet me and was really kind and respectful. He asked for her hand directly, confidently and sincerely. He let me in on when he was going to pop the question and made sure I was in the boat to take pictures. He treats her like the queen she is. He has such resolve and has already navigated so many trials. He is a thinker, smarter than most and laughs in this silly way. He is quirky, mostly when he is only with her. He tells his son fun stories and is an incredible dad. He works so hard for his family, chooses well and leads by leaning into Christ.

My grand boy

No words really for how much I love this boy. It's incredible that you don't even know this little human and instantly love them more than you can describe or imagine. I would do anything for him, he looks at me and knows this fact. His finger holding, open kiss, sound and belly puts me over the edge. The moment he recognized my voice, I literally lost my mind I was so overwhelmed with love for him. Distance is hard, my love for him is fierce.

Chapter 6
Ohana

Ohana means family in Hawaiian. It has always been a word that makes me feel at home. Aloha brings the same feeling to me, this word means breath of life. We were recently in Hawaii and were told that they greet each other by leaning in with their heads and breathing into one another. It is pretty cool.

We don't get to see each other in my family very often, we live all over. I find it fascinating the way some families live near each other and can take each other for granted. One of the benefits of a unique upbringing is that the appreciation for truly healthy, encouraging family members is powerful. In my family, it takes great effort to visit and see people since we are so spread out. Because of this we truly appreciate every minute that we get to see each other. We spend quality time on vacations whenever we can and we try to schedule the next visit before saying goodbye. Goodbyes can be tough.

Breath of Life.

Tragedies also tend to bind unlikely family members together. When my eldest brother passed, I wanted to make sure that my middle brother and I knew each other better. Also, it was very hard on me to spend special occasions like his birthday without people who knew my eldest brother. It helped the grieving process to be around those who knew and loved him. Now after 15 years of taking these trips and connecting, I know my niece, nephews and brother's family much better, it is an absolute gift that I know them more than I perhaps would have. It is a way to honor my eldest brother's memory by knowing those he loved so much and loving them as well.

If you have lost any one close to you or nearly lost them, I hope you purposefully think about how it might be healing to lean into the painful feelings and see what beauty can come from it.

Sicknesses can have a similar effect, I've seen when a family member is ill or gets injured and a family all flies in and it can feel a bit overwhelming. Knowing the best way to help an individual by asking them honors them. Asking questions such as, should we stagger our visits or all come together? The person who is going through the tough stuff may not know exactly how they need help, however they will feel more respected and supported if you respect them enough to ask them.

> *Knowing the best way to help an individual by asking them honors them.*

Listening and supporting your loved ones always comes first, then there is a time for practical needs and help. When you feel that time is at hand below are a few questions that can help with family and friends who are like family in difficult times:

1) How can I best support you right now?
2) Would you like me to come there now, in a week, in a month? (if you live far away)
3) Would you like to come here for a while?
4) Is there something that is really hard for you to do that I can help with? (the answer here may surprise you, each person grieves and deals with hardships in a unique way, be sure to take their request seriously and handle gently)
5) Where are you at today? (This is a bit better than how are you, because it helps the experience be temporary and they can answer in a way that expresses pain without living in it for a moment)
6) Would you like me to call you or come by every Wednesday? (various day that is a regular check in)
7) Would you like me to watch your kids/grandkids for a bit so you can have a breather?

Individuals who do this well, help you feel like you are helping them by allowing them to help in some way. They don't make you feel like it's a burden. Be persistent and caring, express if you aren't sure how to help but are certain you want to. Honesty goes a great deal in all interactions, however in hard situations it is absolutely the most important.

If you're loved one is in the hospital, I would recommend however possible to be by their side. Although doctors and nurses do their absolute best, there are many patients and if you are there to keep track of the details, mistakes can be reduced. Also, don't be afraid to call your closest friends to help with some shifts. When my loved one was in the hospital, two of my closest friends supported me by coming and visiting or taking care of the hard conversations with certain individuals that I just wasn't up to having.

When another loved one was in the hospital, my family and I split time making sure that we were with during different parts of recovery. Just knowing you aren't in the situation alone, is worth its weight in gold, and this is what Ohana is all about really.

Just knowing you aren't in the situation alone, is worth its weight in gold, and this is what Ohana is all about really.

There are individuals who feel as close as family but aren't blood. These individuals feel like you've always known them and always will. There is a curiosity about legacy that is super charged. To know people and places in a deep way, share woes and heart aches, joys, they relationships are precious. The stuff of life pales in comparison when the relationships of your life are rich. To be truly accepted, warts and all is something of beauty. Sometimes it takes creating a family a part from your biological family to help you love those who are blood better. "Be excellent to each other and to your ship," is a saying that I recently heard. I also like the saying to treat your friends like family and family like friends, that keeps respect and love at the forefront as opposed to getting too comfortable. We tend to take those closest to us for granted.

One of the silver linings of life altering events, such as major health issues, deaths and wake-up calls is that they help us to refocus on what's important. Each day is absolutely a gift.

Each day is absolutely a gift.

Saying no well is something I am just learning and knowing how to kindly say both yes and no whole heartedly to your family is absolutely key. One of the examples that I watched of this displayed was when I was co-facilitating a grief share class. A spouse had just died after many months of battling cancer, all of their adult children had been together most of the day and night. The surviving spouse overheard the children starting to talk about who would sleep where. Very gently the surviving spouse said to them that they all could go home, as they normally would have. I loved the way what the surviving spouse needed was the most important, the children were honored without compromising healing. Such a gift to be real, authentic and love enough to say what you need.

Such a gift to be real, authentic and love enough to say what you need.

God has this incredible way of bringing people into your life to help offset hurts and broken relationships with key roles in your life. For instance, if a parent isn't especially close to you, believes strongly differently or is no longer a part of your life, God can bring in a God Momma or Pappa who helps ease the loss. This person generally is someone who you feel a comfort with that is not earthly. It's someone who you just know God has placed into your life.

One of the first times I felt this it was at a dear friends house before she was a dear friend. I had just dropped by, which I never do and we ended up talking for hours about all of our woes, praying together and focusing on God. I left her house with several books that only God could have known I needed. He led me to her to hear something I needed to hear, in a place of safety with a God-honoring woman who still to this day is one of my favorite prayer warriors.

Relationships at their core are special not trivial. It isn't expected that you are going to be best friends with every single person and knowing when you feel a connection, is really part of paying attention to when to step on a lily pad and when to avoid one.

Relationships at their core are special not trivial.

Seek every step with prayer and trust what you feel like after and during your encounters with people. I am an individual who really doesn't like gossip, to my core I avoid it and don't engage in it. However, I also have learned there are certain situations that I should have spoken-up about. This is a process. Learning how to set boundaries in your life is critically important for you and your families best. Boundaries can be absolutely key especially when there is a history of concern. One boundary I've heard of is when there has been abusive patterns between a parent and their child and that child has children, the children are not allowed to go to their grandparents. This way there is a boundary protecting against repeated abuse. This solution set an expectation for the relationship that protected the children, while honoring the parent to have some role in their lives. I thought it was really important and have made similar decisions in my own life. If someone is unkind to me when its just us two, I avoid being alone with that person.

I avoid being alone with that person.

Changing relationships particular with family can be tough. However, if you have sought good counsel, taken it to the Lord, and truly humbled yourself in the situation, sometimes change is necessary. Approaching the change with honesty and communicating effectively, even if the family member doesn't want to hear it, is very important. We cannot respond for our family members and they will respond in ways that we may not like. However, their response is up to them, our ability to communicate in a kind honest way is up to us.

The last couple lily pads that I will highlight are individuals who I know God has clearly placed to support me. I've highlighted each of the ways they've supported me with one key word.

Fearless - I have incredible individuals who are always challenging me, encouraging me to get outside of my comfort zone. Believing in me so fiercely, saying you are amazing. There is nothing you can't do. Bringing me words, treats, picking me up and loving me so well.

Love - I have a man who believes I walk on water. He seeks God's wisdom of how to cherish me and my family while ensuring he is acting with the utmost integrity. To say I am giving love a second chance through his incredible woo'ing and courting of me, is not an overstatement. He calls me his best friend and we are so kind to each other. I love us.

Inspiration - I have individuals who God has placed who show me how to be a better me, how to seek the good no matter what. How to be wise in the hardest of situations and to move on even in the midst of hurt. It is such a gift to watch individuals who inspire you by just being who they are.

Printed in the United States
By Bookmasters